BELIEVE!
A Collection of Faith Poems

by
JUDGE J. ROBERT STUMP (Ret.)

BELIEVE!
A Collection of Faith Poems

Copyright 2015
By J. Robert Stump

All rights reserved, including the right to reproduce, transmit, store, perform or record the contents hereof.

Written by Judge J. Robert Stump (Ret.)

ISBN: 978-1-937641-95-5

"I urge you to read Judge Robert Stump's book *Believe!–A Collection of Faith Poems*. Once you have read this powerful little book, you will want to read it again and again, just as I did."

DON M. GREEN
Executive Director
The Napoleon Hill Foundation

"Please take the opportunity to read Judge Bob Stump's labor of love. I believe you will find this book thought provoking and inspirational."

TAMI ELY
Interim Vice Chancellor for
Development & College Relations
The University of Virginia's College at Wise

"As we age and face our destiny we tend to become more reflective, spiritual, and ponder our legacy. These poems are the legacy of a spiritually mature individual who has not only pondered his legacy, but has created it. Using poetry he addresses the truths, the parables, the miracles, the warnings, and the promises found in the Bible. One immediately recognizes the completeness of the work and perhaps views the Bible in a somewhat different light."

DR. PRESTON D. MILLER, JR., DDS
Clinical Professor Division of Periodontics
Medical University of South Carolina

"Read this little book with celestial advice:
Ponder each phrase more than twice–
Pure pregnant purpose meanings,
Cause compulsive Christ-like cleansings!"

The Divine message of *"Believe!"* is:

"Believe in Christ, Achieve the perfect afterworld, a better place in which to live."

Jesus said:

"These words you hear are not my own; they belong to the Father who sent me."
JOHN 14:24

In Christ,
J. Robert Stump ✝

INTRODUCTION AND ACKNOWLEDGMENTS

I was an English and Latin major in college, an avid reader of novels, books, later the law, secretly, "a wannabe poet," and then a lawyer, judge, and mediator for 50 years. In my retirement, I wanted to write books about my experiences in the courtroom (they are many; the good, the bad, the ugly and humorous—I may still do it, God willing). But three years ago, God directed me to study the Bible and read more than 150 religious/Christian books relating to Biblical issues, controversies, proofs, beliefs, Christian attitudes and opinions, et al. Then, He inspired me to put these beliefs and issues into rhyming poetry for the loving, seeking mind to believe in His Son.

I have dedicated **Believe!** to the Holy Trinity: God, Jesus Christ and the Holy Spirit as solitary one. They looked over my shoulder, guided my mind and hand spiritually in choosing the rhyming words herein. Believe and trust His message, not mine. The sole purpose of these poems is to plant the seed in your heart, and convert you to a Christ Believer! Thank you, Lord! Amen!

My tolerant, loving, understanding, forgiving, inspiring, intellectual, common sense, supporting wife for 48 years, Alice Marrs Stump, has been my guiding light with her frankness, strength, courage, wisdom, and ability to keep my feet on the ground during my life adventure. I love you always and thank you, "Poofie!"

My sincere appreciation to Sheila Shupe, my court/legal secretary for 28 years, who typed these inspired rhymes on The First Baptist Church of Norton's computer and printer. After my continuous changing, and editing, she patiently, and efficiently typed thousands of words over and over again. Thanks, Sheila!

I also give credit for the publication of **Believe!** to Tami Ely, the Interim Vice Chancellor for UVa's College at Wise, VA and Don

Green, Executive Director of the Napoleon Hill Foundation located on the campus at UVa-Wise. They believed, supported me and made this book possible. Thanks, Tami and Don!

I also acknowledge and thank my childhood/lifetime friends, the "Bonded Burton (High School) Brothers" of 70 years, who by their "peer pressure," intelligence, excellent achievements in college and graduate school educations have inspired and motivated me to learn and reach for the highest stars. They are Christ Believers, financial investors, and believers of this book's publication. God bless you, and thanks, Bonded Brothers:

Dr. John D. Fulton, Ph.D, a retired Dean of several universities, and math professor at Clemson University, S.C.; Dr. Charles H. Henderson, M.D., radiologist and medical professor at the University of Virginia, Charlottesville, VA; Dr. Preston D. Miller, Jr., D.D.S., professor of stomatology at MSC University, Charleston, S.C., "the father of periodontics"; and Dr. William P. Kanto, Jr., M.D., professor of pediatrics-neonatology, and Senior Dean for Clinical Affairs, School of Medicine, Medical College of Georgia, Augusta, GA. In the Bonds!

I also must acknowledge the authors of the Christian books I read for their inspiration, knowledge, research and Bible reliability as follows:

All the Bible authors, The Bible, William Paul Young, Lee Strobel, Kyle Idelman, Bill Wiese, Dr. Charles Stanley, Dr. Billy Graham, Joel Rosenberg, David Limbaugh, C.S. Lewis, Raymond A. Moody, Jr. Jim Bishop, Stephen Mansfield, Bill O'Reilly, Steven K. Scott, Phillip Yancey, D. James Kennedy, John Hagee, Rick Warren, Tim Lehayne, Chris Mitchell, Rice Broocks, Wayne Jacobsen, Ron Phillips, Reza Aslan, inter Alia.

Any errors herein blame me, not God. Enjoy God's poems and Believe in His Son!

                          In Christ,
                          J. Robert Stump †
                          1112 Virginia Avenue N.W.
                          Norton, VA 24273
                          May, 2015

BELIEVE!
A Collection of Faith Poems

The last words of Jesus Christ at His ascension:
*"He that believes . . . shall be saved;
but he that does not believe shall be damned."*
MARK 16:16 (KJV)

CONTENTS

Innocent Youthful Query 1

BIBLE BELIEFS

God Exists 5
The Bible is True 8
The Creation–In the Beginning 10
Adam–Being First 12
The Holy Trinity 13
The Law 14
We Already Know 16
Insatiability 18
Idolatry 19
Joseph's Son 22
Holy Conception 23
Jesus: Born of a Virgin 24
The Greatest Story for Children 25
Jesus' Miracles 28
The Trial 29
Jesus Died on the Cross 31
Why Have You Forsaken Me? 36

The Resurrection 38
Life's Mission! To Die 40
If Christ Not Born 41
The Prodigal Son(s) 44
The Good Samaritan 46
The Test – Abraham 47
Job – The Bet 50
The Soil Seed Sower 52
Don't Worry 53
The Wicked Tenants 54
The Marriage Feast 56
The Pearl 58
The Net 59
Rich Fool 60
The Rapture 61
End Times Prophecy 62
Summit Summary 65

PERSONAL BELIEFS

My Humble Daily Prayer 69
Thanksgiving Day Prayer 71
Christmas Crunch 72
Trilogy Analogy 74
The Calendar 75
Truth 76
The Door 78
A Prayer for Help 79
Forgiveness 80
Repentance 81

Love	82
Suicide	83
Forbidden Sex	84
Begin Again	87
Faith – Believe!	88
Fan or Follower?	89
Grace	90
When Bad Things Happen to Good People	92
The Ticket to Heaven	95
Keys to the Kingdom	97
It's Never Too Late	99
Good -v- Evil	100
The Alternative	102
The Afterlife	103
Heaven -v- Hell	104
A Vision of Hell	106
What To Do If Left Behind	109
Believe!	111
How to Believe!	112

DEDICATION

Believe! is dedicated to God, The Holy Spirit and Christ - Inspired by the Holy Trinity with Divine Advice -

Author – Poet
J. Robert Stump ✝
1112 Virginia Avenue N.W.
Norton, Virginia 24273
1-276-275-9365
jrstump@yahoo.com

INNOCENT YOUTHFUL QUERY

The four year old was playing with the three.
They were having fun, what an age to be.
The four year old's name was Mary Beth,
While the three was called Elizabeth.
Two sweet innocent girls,
Both with blonde cute little curls.
One said, "Play like you are dead."
"And I will go to Heaven," the other said.
"No, you will go to Jesus," she replied.
"My momma told me, he's the one who died."
"Who is Jesus?" the four year old queried.
"I don't know," the three year old worried . . . Penned 1976

Does the above poem apply to you?
At your age there is something you can do!
Ponder the following rhyming odes.
Discover who Jesus is – thru Biblical roads.
Was and is Jesus real?
Open your loving heart and feel!
Jesus Christ was the most important man ever on Earth!
His perfect life and words, the best example for our living worth -
Speak to Him now; do yourself the final favor -
Accept Jesus Christ as your personal savior.
Have faith, not doubt, and Jesus receive.
If you care about your afterlife, its urgent you believe! . . . Penned 2015

BIBLE BELIEFS

GOD EXISTS

God is invisible!
He's never appeared to man recognizable.
Envisioned as a burning bush, a voice, or a cloud,
Observed only thru the person of Jesus Christ, His Son so proud.

A god who does not show himself raises doubts.
Join the club of rational well-thought-outs.
Can man have faith in what he has not seen?
Believers tell us He is real, not a dream.

Christians absolutely insist
Atheists can't prove God does not exist.
An informed decision based on evidence
Declares it more reasonable to accept God with confidence.

If you accept the Bible as true,
God revealed Himself to the world and you.
Since man's beginning, God left His fingerprints
Thru millions of peoples' experienced events.

The miraculous universe had a beginning.
It's not logical that something came from nothing.
Something or someone had to cause creation.
Common sense dictates a personal creator's application.

All mankind historically desire a supernatural deity –
Which is the best argument for God's existing integrity.
On this Earth satisfaction gratifies our desires,
Food, water, sex fulfills our fires,
But man made for another eternal world assures our priors.

The complex universe occurred from nothing with an explosive "Big Bang,"
An absurd theory song the atheists sang.

The orderly universe and living humans, they say,
Were born from chaos, by chance, a random accidental birthday.

Christians argue the Earth is an intricate design
To allow precise human life to exist for all-time.
Design implies an intellectual architect,
A personal God like creator producing perfect.

Millions of stars, galaxies, sun, moon, Earth: the universe,
Positioned with precision to sustain life first
Mandates a caused beginning by a supreme being.
The only logical common sense answer is God all doing.

Only God can explain how our living body does exist,
Why our organs, eyes, brain, nervous system, each other assist.
Man could not be born by chance or accident –
Our perfect coordinated body was built by a God designer, brilliant.

Where did moral standards originate?
Not our personal preferences to tolerate,
But by our measure of right and wrong to motivate –
Dictated by a supreme being, God, to illuminate.

How did perfect human life begin?
A fine tuned machine formed over and over again.
A DNA cell can't assemble itself from chemicals at once by chance.
A living cell had to be a product of purposeful intelligence.

Throughout history millions of people claim
A conscious relationship with God:
Despite great sacrifice, even death.
Many trusted Him with their tortured dying breath.
Darwin's evolution theory fails the "survival of the fittest" test –
His survivors would not risk death for their faith (in God), we attest.

How things are perceived from our personal experience

Is an analytical reason to believe God has a true existence.
We can't honestly prove beyond all doubt God is a reality,
But the evidence conclusively concludes God is an actuality.

You are a risk taker with an eternal choice;
If you don't believe God exists, you will not rejoice
Because your soul will burn in the fires of hell.
If you believe God exists, your perpetual afterlife, in Heaven will dwell!

THE BIBLE IS TRUE

We can prove beyond a reasonable doubt
That the Bible is God's inspired word throughout.
Unique unity, fulfilled prophecies, archeological confirmation and early acceptance
Verify it is 99.9% accurate, supported by confident evidence.

The Bible mandates actual truth, not a lie!
It claims to be an unerring superhuman book, not shy!
More than 100 Bible verses quote: "the Lord said,"
Spoken by the Holy Spirit of God, the celestial figurehead.

The Bible recites mythical, miracle, historical, prophetic events
Frequent factual eye witness accounts represent,
And affirm the truth, the whole truth, and nothing but the truth
Heaven-sent, can't deny it's reality to sustain our eternal youth.

The Bible had 40 different authors written over 1500 years
By shepherds, fishermen, rabbis, kings, prophets, a doctor, a variety of careers.
The Bible states clearly it is the inspired word of God Himself –
"God breathed," divinely composed thru man itself.

God chose His authors' individual personalities,
Delicate, distinct, dictating styles and points of view portray His realities.
The Bible's oneness of spiritual purpose is without error,
The Bible books evenly expand and explain the Christian Era.

The Bible is not absolutely mistake free –
Approximations, paraphrasing, appearances, opinions, contradictions still agree
With the overall unified message concurring in its accuracy.
Diverse eye witness observations are accepted as un-conspired fact in legal literacy.

Fulfilled prophecies attest the best argument of the Bible book.
The nations, names, persons, places, events, the total outlook,
Predicted prophecies hundreds of years before the fact,
Affirming God's inspired credible words, later executed exact.

Bible prophecies in the Old Testament came true in the New Testament.

One perfect example was Jesus Christ's fulfillment –
The place, time, manner of His virgin birth,
The betrayal, reaction, burial tomb, manner and purpose of His death worth.

The Bible, 66 books, 40 separate writers, one inspired authorship,
Penned across 1500 years in deserts, cities, and dungeon's death grip.
A single symbolic unified doctrine of faith, morals and salvation.
Each Bible book, a piece of the perfect puzzle, fit the revelation,
Lead by a solitary designer mind – God, complete scripture unification.

Strong evidence of the Bible's authenticity
Is the early acceptance of Christ's message, proving veracity.
Five weeks after Jesus' resurrection and restoration,
Ten thousand Jews changed their faith and joined the Christian congregation.

Jesus' disciples wrote the gospel books within 25 years, accepting
Early belief, since witnesses, survivors and skeptics still living.
Cover-ups are eventually uncovered.
However, the disciples did not recant while being tortured.

Archaeology in modern days have strengthened the external corroboration of
    Biblical reliability.
The gospels affirmed the historical names and locations of countries and
    cities un-deniability.
No example of archaeological excavations and 'facts' discovered.
Have disproved Bible historical events or places uncovered.

You have choices – two:
Believe the Bible is true,
Or that it is untrue!
Which faith is your point of view?

Be aware the risk you do,
If you choose to misconstrue,
Your eternal life will miscue.
Believe the Bible scripture is true, and renew!

THE CREATION–
IN THE BEGINNING

Thousands of years ago,
Before time was measured so
There should have been something,
But there was absolutely nothing.

Existence appeared as a dark vapor
Governed by the Almighty Creator.
All was void without sound,
Pure perfect tranquility all around.

Reality was an exclusive nullity.
Alone, God made the majestic mortality.
The Divine Concept was revealed,
Which previously had been concealed.

Darkness prevailed, obscure and opaque,
Generate light, illuminate and wake.
Thus, He formed the first day with ease,
And with His skill was pleasantly pleased.

On the second day:
He disbursed the misty vapors on high,
And shaped the spectacular sacred sky.
Then, He originated the powerful overflowing ocean,
Where moisture moved in mighty motion.

On the third day:
As if moulding clay in His huge hands,
He created Earth from dusty dry lands.
Water welled up into flowing seas
As did grass, seed bearing plants and living trees.

On the fourth day:
God hung the sun and moon to light the sky,
Placed the stars to preside, guide and identify.
The seasons separated into warm and freeze,
With the division of night and day, again He was pleased.

On the fifth day:
He filled the waters full of fish and swimming things,
And the skies with birds and beating wings.
Frogs and fowl without natural birth,
Reproduced, multiplied, and adorned the earth.

On the sixth day:
Great beasts and lizards arose to shake the ground,
While wild animals emerged to pierce peaceful sound.
Then, He created man in his own image, an innovative birth
As the master of all living creatures on the new Earth.

On the seventh day:
Exhausted, God sat down to rest
For His creation was the glorious best.
It was good and He was finally pleased,
But He feared the mysteries He had released.

ADAM–BEING FIRST

Alone in the new world without companion or a son,
Holy solitary experiment, His creative work begun.
Peaceful silence without a single voice,
Conceiving original being, born of free choice.

The Almighty countenance creating miracle birthright,
Reflecting in the sparkling stream a sacred sight.
Self portrait of misty image form
Painted in the mirrored water yet unborn.

Sculpturing arms, legs, head, fingers and toes,
As well as hands, feet, organs, nerves and nose.
Forming eyes, nails, naked bone and hair,
Adding mind and soul for loving care.

Wonderment appearing: Blood gushing, heart pounding,
Ears listening, nostrils twitching, eyes squinting,
Flesh feeling, fingers touching, chest heaving,
Body breathing, mind thinking, voice sputtering.

Inhaling the last dust from the dormant mouth,
Blowing kiss of life beyond lips into drouth.
"Welcome to the new world without a mother,
Adam, my first son and twin brother."

THE HOLY TRINITY

The Holy Trinity we recall:
God loves us all;
Jesus also loves you;
The Holy Spirit loves you too.
Love God and His Son
Until eternity is done.
Have faith in all three.
United in truth will make you free.

God, Jesus and the Holy Spirit, the Divine Three.
Equal, indivisible, only one for you and me.
Like fog over an icy lake,
Each entity is water for Heaven's sake.
The Father is in Jesus, and He is in Him.
Also the Holy Spirit, the unseen witness without sin.
Each has separate duties to be done.
All three are solitary one.

THE LAW

Sacrilegious seeds flaunt and grow.
If you devote yourself to the Satanic foe.
Adore only one God with praises so,
And worship no earthen alter ego!

God is a jealous God, prevailing.
Make for yourself no idol of anything.
Love others best, but love God most, comparing.
Worship only God, everlasting.

Cleanse your mouth of all profane.
Hold your sinful tongue in chain.
Suffer His wrath and certain pain,
If you take the name of God in vain!

Rest is decreed for all, I say,
Don't toil the seventh for greedy pay.
Therefore this covenant you must obey:
Keep holy the Sabbath Day!

Family loyalty you shall discover,
Devotion to parents as if a lover,
Paternal issue shall serve no other,
Honor your father and your mother!

God's canons are inherently real.
Enshrine His laws and so appeal.
Abide by them with humble kneel.
Renew the pledge: Thou shall not steal!

Control heated hatred if you will.
Premeditated malice is a transitory thrill.
Restrain your wrath and keep it still.

Pray, thou shall not kill!

Affirm the marriage vows, and never quit.
Marital harmony, you will admit.
Don't be unfaithful not a little bit.
Adultery, thou shall not commit!

Misrepresent the truth, you never should.
Acknowledge your brother with everlasting good!
Substitute yourself in the place he stood.
Don't bear your neighbor any falsehood!

Be modest and meek as a mouse!
Don't let greed transform you to a louse!
Thou shall not covet thy neighbor's house,
Nor covet thy neighbor's spouse!

WE ALREADY KNOW

We already know,
But some refuse to accept it so!

The words of Jesus are hard for us to accept,
Because we too often seek our peer's respect.
If we follow His teachings in our everyday life,
We will be reduced to simple poverty and strife.

Our society teaches us to adore expensive things,
And all the power and influence a successful job brings.
Advertisements praise our ownership of fancy cars,
And we idolize the jet set Hollywood stars.

We need the biggest and best houses in town;
Attend the finest schools and social clubs around.
We must wear the latest labeled clothes
With jewelry and furs from head to toes.

We must eat at all the proper places,
And drop the names of famous faces.
Compelled to associate with the powerful winners,
Whether politicians, leaders or respected sinners.

Who are we trying to impress?
Inside ourselves we must confess!
We are searching for false securities,
When we accumulate all those personal impurities.

We do our good deeds because they are seen,
When our true intent is not so clean.
We try to prove our merits to our peers,
Waiting for their acceptance and applauding cheers.

The exalted shall be humbled, and the reverse is true;
For the humbled shall be exalted, it can happen to you.
We, already know,
But some refuse to accept it so!

Declare your freedom and accept the risk of revelation!
Be brave as our forefathers who founded our nation.
Spiritual freedom will allow us to breathe anew,
If we seek possessions and praises, but a few.

Cast away all those expensive pretty toys,
And gather in simple pleasures and peaceful joys.
Because all we need is understanding and love—
The perfect and purest gift from our God above!

We already know,
But some refuse to accept it so!

INSATIABILITY

Wealth is true goal – from youth we are told;
Stop at nothing, be bold – affluence will unfold.
Why do we want it? – Because it is there.
Once we get it – we don't really care.

Govern all power – toil hour by hour;
Evade nervous cower – achieve the highest tower.
Why do we want it? – Because it is there.
Once we get it – we don't really care.

Consume all cuisine – lick your plate clean;
Eat every nutrient seen – devour like epicurean.
Why do we want it? – Because it is there.
Once we get it – we don't really care.

Subdue sexual intercourse – carnal knowledge of course;
Gratify with force – be passionate and amorous.
Why do we want it? – Because it is there.
Once we get it – we don't really care.

Restore health and vitality – physical and mental reality;
By-pass body abnormality – guarantee immortality.
Why do we want it? – Because it is there.
Once we get it – we don't really care.

Temperance in all things best – a mediocre test;
Middle of the road blessed – build a median nest.
Why do we want it? – Because it is there.
Once we get it – we don't really care.
 . . . . or do we?

IDOLATRY

You shall have no other gods before me – 1st Commandment.
Make no idols of worship before Me of anything. 2nd Commandment -
Love others and things best, but love God most, the pecking order.
Worship only God, the everlasting titleholder.

What are worshiping images and idols?
First thoughts are: statue-like golden models.
But a false idol is anything we sacrifice for and pursue,
Like appetite, addiction, ambition, amusement, no enduring value.

False idols crave: food, sex, entertainment,
Pleasure goals for our self-attainment.
We desire false idols of money, success, achievement
To pursue our **power** of self-improvement.

False idols put: romance, family, self-pride of me
Above the **Love** of God, The Deity.
False idols are anything that replace
God in our lives for our self-disgrace.

Idolatry is adultery ultimately portrayed,
Rejecting God as "The Lover Betrayed."
God is jealous, so glorify His Love, do not depart.
Love and worship Him first with all your heart.

Pleasure

Food is a **pleasure** false-idol, obese people cannot defeat.
Some eat to live, others live to eat.
God will provide your bread of life.
Trust Him to feed your soul. Put down that butter knife.

Sex is a *pleasure* false-idol, resulting in temporary satisfaction and emptiness,
Causing mental pain, separation, divorce and loneliness.
Pray Godly thoughts, "Deliver me from the Evil One."
Choose an intimate relationship with Jesus, The Holy Son.

Entertainment and amusement, false-idols, are *pleasure* obsessions,
Such as sports, video games, the internet, T.V., temporal digressions.
Enjoying captivating creature comforts like a meaningless orgy.
Our hearts are restless until they find tranquil peace in HE.

Power

Success is a *power* false-idol, "I'm king of ambition and pride."
Your choice: "I can do it all myself," or let Jesus decide.
It's not good to conquer the whole nation,
Yet forfeit your soul to evil damnation.

Money is the ultimate *power* false-idol, "The root of all evil."
Worshiping the almighty dollar leads to immoral upheaval.
We are never happy nor satisfied, we want more and more.
Enjoy God's praise, give all your money to the poor.

Achievement is also a *power* false-idol, comparing ourselves to others.
We always compete to win against our brothers.
Don't measure and frustrate yourself by what others think of you.
Concern yourself only with what Jesus thinks you do.

Love

Romance is a *love* false-idol, sentimental companionship.
Loving our spouse is the best romantic intimate relationship.
But God wants us to love and worship Him the most.
Worship and adore Him as a father foremost.

Family is a *love* false-idol, as a father loves his son the best.
Abraham chose God over his son and passed the love test.
God so loved the world He gave His only Son to amend.
He sacrificed His Son to save all sinners at world's end.
There is no greater love than one who died for a friend.

The god of me is the worst *love* false-idol, its all about you.
Some believe they are god-like, perfect and true,
Afraid to fail with an arrogant point of view.
Choose God over me, myself and I, and others too.

Instead of creating your own *pleasure, power,* and *love,*
Return to God as a secure source above.
Idolatry is substituting anything but God for your stress and thirst for release.
Drink from Jesus first and you'll enjoy hopeful peace.

JOSEPH'S SON!

Chaste mate
Maiden celibate
Betrothed with child
Body not defiled.

Fiancé without blame
Her child he could not claim
Quietly divorced from the scene
Drifted into a dream.

An angel appeared in a vision:
"The Lord sent you on this mission.
Do not fear to take her as your wife –
It is the destiny of your life."

God's message from the prophets bring
A virgin shall conceive an offspring
The Holy Spirit within her womb
Sinners saved at the tomb.

Earthly Father doth ordain.
Prepare Him for a saintly reign
Immanuel is "God with us."
Name Him Baby Jesus.

HOLY CONCEPTION

The faithful believe
How she did conceive.
Engaged to be married,
Holy Son she carried.
Her husband to be,
Joseph of Galilee.

Ripe red cherry,
Virtuous virgin Mary.
Her awe of what might be,
Trust the Lord in thee.
Sanctuary where no man trod,
Favored lady of God.

Ageless King shall reign,
Miracle no man can explain.
Woman's womb so cold,
Birth of Jesus foretold.
Pure pregnant prodigy,
Eternal Christian theology.

JESUS: BORN OF A VIRGIN

Seven hundred years or so before Jesus' birth,
God declared His Son would miraculously enter Earth.
Isaiah prophesied a virgin would bear a son,
His name would be "Immanuel," the perfect one.

The angel said to Mary: "the Holy Spirit will come upon you,
And the power of the most high will overshadow you
. . . . the holy offspring shall be the Son of God,
. . . . for nothing is impossible with God!"

From the day He was born until the day He died,
Jesus was perfect without sin until crucified.
To be a perfect sacrifice without sin.
He himself must be perfect without sin.

Virgin birth is a supernatural act of God's love,
A miracle created by an omnipotent God above.
A birth without sexual relations, an unbelievable fate
Unless a miracle occurs as the historical gospels state.

Faith requires belief without sight or touch.
Common sense can exist without fact so much.
A miracle is hard to conceive –
Unless with your loving heart you believe!

THE GREATEST STORY FOR CHILDREN

On December 24 a long time ago –
A man and his wife, Mary and Joe
Traveled far to a distant land –
Mary, pregnant, rode on a donkey, while Joe held her hand.

The little donkey had a sparkling red nose,
And was lively and quick from his head to his toes.
It was his magical duty to carry them –
To the little town of Bethlehem.

Mary wore a pure white flowing gown –
That was unsoiled and did not touch the ground.
Her purpose was for all the world to please,
As her long silky hair blew in the breeze.

It was late and they were tired and spent,
But the motel owner had no rooms to rent.
He did have a stable near the barn,
Which lacked much class or simple charm.

It had been occupied before by a large white horse,
Who had left his natural scent of course.
A few pigs, a lamb and cow
Were asleep on the hay even now.

Even though the stable was smelly and unkempt,
Mary and Joe were quietly content,
For tonight was the big event,
Which brought them to this wooden tent.

Meanwhile in a far off town,
There was a crazy king with a jeweled crown.
Herod was his name,
And meanness was his game.

He heard that a new king was to be born,
So he was jealous and full of scorn.
He sent Three Wise ole' Men to find
The new born king, who would be so kind.

But King Herod had a black cold heart,
And wanted to cut the new born king apart.
But the Three Wise Men had no intent
To lead the mean old king to the wooden tent.

A star shown bright in the sky,
That appeared to rise up on high.
It glowed and sparkled just like day,
And led their path to the manger and hay.

It was early morning on December twenty-five,
When the new baby king was born alive.
A gold crown hovered above his head –
He was cradled in a wooden straw bed.

His name was Baby Jesus,
And He was sent to please us.
He came to save all of you –
From all the bad things that you do.

Swaddling clothes covered his cute little belly,
And He smelled sweet like honey and jelly.
He had soft blue all knowing eyes,
And looked peaceful and wise.

The Wise Men brought presents to show their respect
For the new Baby King who was perfect.
As they knelt in prayer by the animals in the hay,
They knew their souls were cleansed that day.

Gifts from the Wise Men three.

Teach a happy lesson to you and me.
'Tis the single holy reason –
For our Christmas season.

King Baby Jesus was born because –
There would be no other purpose for Santa Claus.
Now you know why you get toys on Christmas Day.
It's in memory of Christ Jesus' Birthday.

JESUS' MIRACLES

Trust the apostles: Matthew, Mark, Luke and John.
The Bible is not a fabricated con.
Believe the testimony of a 1000 men.
It is a true history of human sin.

Jesus was a loving, merciful, forgiving teacher,
Not a magician, sorcerer, nor bewitching creature.
He radiated a kind, generous, compassionate feature,
An all knowing, enlightened, perceptive preacher.

One wonder factor convinces the clear proof.
The irrefutable miracles of Jesus tell the truth.
No other human so pure –
God's Son for sure!

Jesus changed water into wine –
With 2 fishes, 5 barley loaves He fed 5,000 to dine.
He cured cripples to walk upright,
And restored a blind man's sight.

Jesus healed a child's fever and a withered hand,
Cured a leper, and caused a palsy victim to stand.
He walked on water it was said,
And raised Lazarus and others from the dead.

The Bible declares only one (blasphemy) unpardonable sin –
Attributed to the Pharisees way back when.
They said Jesus' miracles came from Satan's force,
When in fact the Holy Spirit was the true source!

Through the power of the Holy Spirit Jesus pleads.
No other human performed such amazing deeds.
These shocking wonders did not arise from Satan's tent.
Jesus' marvelous miracles were God sent.

THE TRIAL

The Teacher was so great!
No one could imitate.
The Father did create
His purpose in His fate.

'Twas the last time
They would dine.
Body and bread, symbols sublime:
Blood and wine.

Twelve, but a few.
Only one, He knew!
The betrayer askew,
Envy in the Jew.

Agony and prayer!
Disciples slept without a care.
A prophet, but always fair.
A perfect plot portrayer there.

Stand before the High Priest.
False accusations from the beast.
Silent answers increase.
Saint with peculiar peace.

A loathsome legal mess.
For He had confess.
The Messiah? Yes!
Death verdict, you guess!?

Pilate, governor and judge.
Roman law did fudge.
The mob refused to budge.

An innocent man; He had no grudge.

Blood spilled on sorrow sands.
Pontius Pilate washed his hands.
The angry crowd cried its cold demands.
Carry out the cruel commands.

Let the murderer go!
Crucify the fabled foe!
Nail His hand and toe!
Sanctify and sow!

Are those horns?
No! A crown of thorns!
Son of God adorns.
Save all the unborns!

JESUS DIED ON THE CROSS

Was Jesus' death a fake?
A fraud or trick for Heaven's sake?
His legendary death 2000 years ago,
Cause us to ponder the problem so.
Did He die or remain alive?
Could crucifixion allow Him to survive?
Did Jesus die, we ask now.
Let's explore the reasons how.
Follow this ancient past tense
With expert medical common sense.
We also need proof from biblical sources
To corroborate our investigative courses.
Keep an open mind
For the answer we seek to find.

First consider gospel facts before torture on the cross.
It was the night before the Jesus loss.
After "The Last Supper," Jesus began to sweat blood.
His next day's crucifixion, He understood.
Jesus knew what the next day would bring –
A horrible beating and the crucifixion thing.
He suffered psychological stresses,
A medical condition, "Hematidrosis," to excesses.
Severe anxiety releases chemicals to flow –
In the sweat glands, tinged with blood, you know.
A side effect made very sensitive His skin,
When the next day's flogging would begin.

After Jesus' "trial," Roman soldiers "scourged" the whip
Made of braided leather thongs and hard grip,
With metal balls woven inside and sharp bones,
It was like a hundred piercing casted stones.
At least 39 lashes plagued His pain,

Laid bare His back, buttocks, back legs again and again,
Exposing His veins, muscles and bowels to the air.
Roman soldiers enjoyed the punishment without care.
The beatings caused "hypovolemic shock."
Loss of much blood by the clock.
His heart raced to pump blood, but there was none,
Blood pressure dropped, He fainted and was almost done.

The kidneys would not produce urine to pass –
Jesus is thirsty and slipping fast.
Lacerations tore skeletal muscles, a mesh;
Producing quivering ribbons of bleeding flesh.
Then Jesus carried the heavy cross thru the town
He fainted, collapsed, and was lying down.
Some victims never made it to the crucifixion,
Instead they early on recited their own benediction.

The Roman guards used spikes 5" to 7" long,
Tapered to a sharp point, they were strong.
They drove nails thru His wrists, not His hands
The median nerves crushed, twisted like rubber bands.
Both His arms stretched 6" in lengthy gain,
Dislocating His shoulders in terrible pain.
Psalm 22, a biblical prophetic point:
The future Messiah's – "Bones out of joint."
His wrists and arms nailed to the horizontal beam,
While His feet nailed to the vertical staked seam.
As Jesus was hoisted up on the crossbar –
The crown of thorns in His head left an ugly scar.
He heavily dangled from the wooden cross with extreme pain.
Nerves, flesh, bones crushed and severed again.

His body hanging vertically down
Slow death by asphyxiation – no holy crown.
Jesus could not exhale without His feet on the ground
Trying to breathe, complete exhaustion all around.

Jesus suffered "respiratory acidosis," a medical feat,
Blood increases, causing an erratic heart beat
Fluid collected in membranes around the heart and lungs,
Causing a rapid heart rate, His inner body like a sponge.
Jesus craved water at first.
He cried from the cross, "I thirst."
A sip of vinegar was offered Him,
But it only dribbled down His chin.
Death was close, there was no doubt.
Jesus knew He was dying, and began to shout:
Forever in eternity with you, I'm near it –
"Lord into thy hands, I commend my spirit."

Then the icing on the cake,
The Roman soldiers did partake.
To confirm the deathly act.
To ratify His end in fact,
The soldier thrust a spear in His side
Into the heart and lungs it did glide.
When the spear was pulled out,
Clear fluid, water and blood, did spout.
The Roman soldiers were expert killers to one –
Their incentive was to get the job done.
For if the victim survived and they failed,
Death was their punishment – not jailed.

If Jesus survived the cross –
His arms and legs were at a loss -
Massive wounds to His back – His fate
Loss of blood in a pathetic state.
He could not breathe,
We logically conceive.

If not dead, Jesus would have barely been alive.
The disciples would have nursed Him to survive.
But soon thereafter He appeared as a healthy human being

Too many witnesses saw this miracle seeming.
How could His disciples and many others
Soon observe Him preaching to His brothers?
His body could not have endured
Such brutal torture He procured.

A new word created by His pain – "excruciating" –
The Latin derivative – "out of the cross" – emanating.
Today our government controls capital punishment to be fair.
We inject poisons and use the electric chair.
But crucifixion was uncontrolled in ancient days.
Death by crude, slow, painful inhuman ways.

Why did Jesus allow Himself to be crucified?
Humiliated, tortured, suffered and tried?
A normal human being would have cried,
And from this tragedy try to hide.
But Jesus knew His sole decision,
Placed on the earth for a holy mission:
To redeem the rebellion against God by all men;
To die for us to save all our sin;
To suffer the death penalty we all dread,
And let us live for eternity instead.
Jesus was motivated by absolute love
From His Holy Father in Heaven above.

Did Jesus die on the cross
To save us from our loss?
A crucifixion victim must ultimately die.
Death cannot be faked or eluded, I do imply.
I believe He died
To save my hide;
Forgive all my sin
Like all other men.
He was resurrected
To insure our eternal life perfected.

I am convinced it is true.
What about you?

". . . . WHY HAVE YOU FORSAKEN ME?"

Theologians for centuries have pondered this mystery –
Jesus' puzzling words on the cross in history.
In despair, He cried out His plea –
"My God, My God, why have you forsaken me?"

What was in Jesus' mind at that dark dreadful moment,
While He suffered humility and frightful torment?
Jesus' speculations may have perceived –
His Father had left Him, He temporarily believed!

At some of our darkest agonizing hours,
We humans believe God has lost His healing powers.
We think He's left us in our dire need.
But in truth, He still loves and is with us indeed.

Jesus experienced the doubts of a human being,
As He sunk to the depths of hell with sinful feeling.
His trust in His Father was temporarily lost,
As He forfeited the true purpose of the cross.

God, the Father, did not abandon His Son;
Only He could finish the holy mission to be done.
A devoted God would not leave His Son alone.
But for all our sins Jesus had to die to atone.

Jesus had absorbed all the wickedness of mankind,
And His human bondage made Him blind.
Jesus became "sin itself" for us,
And this sacrilege obscured Him from His Father's trust.
So utterly black was the deep pit of Jesus' human sin,
He could not clearly see His true calling's end.

But here is the answer and the rest of the story –

Jesus realized and proclaimed the Holy Glory.
Soon after Jesus' abandonment cry –
His Father's trust returned, He did try.
His faith was absolutely restored,
As He gave himself totally to His Lord,
When He shouted – and death He did not fear it –
"Father, into thy hands I commend my spirit."

THE RESURRECTION

Did Jesus Christ return from the dead?
Yes! The Bible and authenticated historical records said!
The core issue of Christianity spread!
The greatest possible miracle: we've read!
If you do not believe Jesus rose from the dead,
Then when you die, you will be eternally dead!
If you believe Jesus died, and then lived again to reign,
He paid your sin-debt, so a new life you will regain!

Analyzing the medical and historical facts,
Jesus could not have survived the crucifixion impacts.
He was flogged, nailed, suffered hypovolemic shock,
His lung and heart were pierced in deadlock.
Roman executioners skillfully killed on the cross and left no victim alive,
Knowing they would die – if the victim did survive.
When all the tortures He suffered are applied,
The ultimate conclusion is: Jesus died!

After His death, Jesus was buried in a tomb.
It's close location was known and guarded by His enemies we presume.
Three days later the tomb was found empty
By His female followers, who had credibility.
Even His adversaries admitted the tomb was vacant –
His body was gone – all agreed, no argument.
The disciples had no motive or opportunity to steal His body away.–
A theory not even the most skeptical critics believe today.

3 to 40 days after His death, eye witnesses saw Jesus living.
Different individuals and groups saw Him walking, eating and breathing.
Hundreds touched Him and heard Him speak.
Early testimony proved He was no mythological, legendary freak.
Unbelievers – Paul, James and Thomas – converted into believers,
When they met Him in person, became faithful receivers.

Critics had time to cross examine witnesses to disprove His living presence.
But the doubters finally confirmed His factual existence.

Jesus' disciples suddenly and sincerely
Changed; and believed He had risen, clearly.
Jesus talked to them in the flesh,
Directed them to preach His message afar and afresh.
The disciples proclaimed worldwide
With glorious, faithful pride
That Jesus, the Son of God, died;
And arose alive from the crucifying homicide.
The disciples were later beheaded, crucified, tortured to die
For their belief in Jesus' resurrection on which they did rely.

Nobody knowingly, willingly and painfully dies for a lie.
Our law doctrine today is: people do not lie,
When they know they are going to die,
And meet their maker in the sky –
A "guarantee of trustworthiness" and credibility,
Even though self-serving, it passes the test of reliability.

Soon after Jesus' resurrection, thousands of Jews
Abandoned their centuries-old religious views;
Believed Jesus was the Son of God and followed Him;
And adopted Christian Communion and Baptism, verbatim.
The resurrection of Christ is the sole conclusion
For Christianity in the face of brutal Roman persecution.
Today two billion Christians believe in Jesus with faithful conviction,
Primarily because of His real resurrection.

LIFE'S MISSION! TO DIE
. . . . ON OUR BEHALF

The most important superior man
In God's created Earth lifespan –
Three reasons set Him apart and reveal,
Jesus Christ's superhuman appeal:

Jesus, "The Messiah," was expected, a pre-announced deity,
Hundreds of years before His entry, His virgin birth, life and death, a prophecy
From ancient antiquity,
Validated by tests of future history and perpetuity.

He appeared with supernatural impact.
Historical time split in two as a matter-of-fact:
Before and after His coming, a precise act,
A.D., "Anno Domini," in the year of our Lord, to be exact.
Even atheists mark His time to attack.

His mission on Earth
Was not His birth,
But to die
For others sins to sanctify,
Purify, satisfy and rectify.

Jesus' death, His life's mission and epitaph:
To die on our behalf.
He was perfect without sin;
Had to be killed to conquer death and sin;
Crucified on the cross to save our wicked skin;
His resurrection granted man's new life to begin again.
. . . . . Amen!

IF CHRIST NOT BORN

If Jesus Christ not born:
The moral world would not perform.
Sinful lives changed? No reform!
Peaceful civilization, forever torn.

Ancient history reveals human life cheap.
Infants, elderly, women, Jews killed like sheep.
Cruel kings, cannibalism, suicide, homicide, slaves made man weep.
Then restraining morals appeared, a quantum leap,
When Christ born, our souls to keep.

Compassion, mercy came from brotherly love
Brought and taught by Christ and God above.
Christian charities save the needy and disable
Give to poor, homeless, widows, orphans and unstable.

Doctors, nurses, hospitals, missionaries, heal the sick
Invented by Christ's miracles, Bible basic.
World without Christ is world without charity.
Giving good healthy life is a Christian verity.

Christ says sex only permitted in marriage morally.
Taking Christ away defeats the American family.
The family unit secures all great nations.
With no Christian moral restraints countries suffer cancellations.

The Lord says, "If anyone will not work, neither shall he eat."
Self-reliance, private enterprise, our society is complete.
Jesus' parables preach money, property and economics,
Teaching capitalism, free enterprise and good work ethics.

America founded by Christ Believers.
Our constitution, bill of rights based on godly lawgivers.

Our government's separation of powers to protect us
Rooted in Biblical: Judge,   laws and King Jesus.
                  (Judiciary) (Legislative) (Executive)
All early American colleges and universities
Created for ministers to spread Christian humanities.
Pioneers of science were Christian leaders.
Physics, chemistry, biology, anatomy evolved from Bible readers.

U.S. freedom of speech and religion would not be concise
Without the greatest civil libertarian, Jesus Christ.
God's laws prohibiting murder, theft, adultery, lies
To protect life, property, marriage, truth adopted by U.S., to civilize.

If no Christ:
Life would have no aim,
Nothing to gain,
No meaning,
No beginning.

If no Christ:
No paradise,
No forgiveness for sin,
No new perfect body to begin again.

If no Christ:
No true freedom from guilt
For sins stupidly spilt.
Only He can remove sinful silt,
Evil lives to be rebuilt.

If no Christ:
There will be pain and tears
For all eternal years.
Only His sacrifice paid arrears.
Belief in Him satisfies fateful fears

If no Christ:
No God in human flesh
To pay for man's sin afresh –
A sin debt
He did not beget.

If no Christ:
The atheists do say,
No promises convey,
Only misery and betray,
No eternal holy day.

If no Christ:
Man can't earn His way
Which good deeds portray.
No perfect life resumé,
Not good enough without Christ, I pray!

If Christ born:
Trust in Jesus –
Shall save us!
Repent all sin –
Live in Heaven! Amen!

THE PRODIGAL SON(S)
A PARABLE OF JESUS

Jesus preached the parable – "The Prodigal Son."
To a group of sinners, tax collectors, clergy, Pharisees all-in-one.
The sinners and tax collectors depict the younger son.
The clergy and Pharisees symbolize the older son.

Jesus spoke: A wealthy father had two sons.
Although the father was not dead, the younger son
Asked for his half share of his dad's inheritance,
So he could journey to a distant country, to explore a new existence.

After several years, the younger son squandered all his share of his father's wealth
On drinking, prostitutes, wild life and bad health.
All his money gone, he took a job feeding pigs in a pig pen.
A famine struck, starving, his needs sunk to a dead end.

The younger son finally awoke to common sense –
"I'm penniless, hungry, even my father's servants eat." Hence,
"I am unworthy," but with my father I'll try to make up.
I will reconcile with him. "So he got up."

The father saw his younger son coming from afar,
And he ran out to greet him, kissed and hugged him like a superstar.
The younger son said, "I have sinned against Heaven and you,"
"Take me back as one of your hired servants, any task I will do."

"My son was lost and is found," the father did narrate.
"Kill the fattened calf, we'll feast and celebrate."
The older son refused to honor his brother's return,
He was jealous, angry and critical of his father's concern.

"I stayed home, worked hard, and obeyed your rule,
And now you want to toast this sinning fool."

He wasted your money on prostitutes. But not me,
"I've been good, I deserve your blessing," you see.

The father patiently explained: "Everything I have is yours."
"You are always with me, you are my guarantor.
Your younger brother was dead and is now alive."
This is the reason we rejoice for he did survive.

The younger son, guilty of insulting choices and reckless living.
The father embraced his return with hugs and forgiving.
The older son spoke harshly to his father with disrespect.
The father lovingly explained himself with grace, patience and self-respect.

The younger son said, "I sinned, I am not worthy," I pray.
The older son said, "I'm good, I've never disobeyed."
This moral tale is a shameful sad song.
Because both sons were absolutely wrong!

The younger brother was lost in his badness.
The older brother was lost in his goodness.
God is not a cosmic cop seeking revenge and controls.
God is a doctor healing hurt lost souls.

Jesus' parable is not about two sons who disobey intentionally,
But about a father who loves his children unconditionally.
Compare this fable to our Godly Father's true love,
Who forgives and welcomes all His sinning children home to Heaven above.

THE GOOD SAMARITAN
A PARABLE OF JESUS

A Jew, traveling a deserted desert road was hijacked.
Bandits stripped, robbed and beat him, a brutal attack.
Left him bleeding on the roadside half-dead.
So Jesus in His parable said.

A priest came by and saw the Jew in pain.
Did not stop to help, and continued on his journey again.
A Levite clergyman approached, by-passed the Jew, and did the same.
Two holy travelers showed no sympathy, full of shame.
Merely abandoning an animal in distress is inhumane.

A Samaritan, traditionally an enemy of a Jew,
Who had pity, mercy and compassion, came to the rescue;
Bandaged and nursed his wounds; carried him on a donkey to a village inn;
And prepaid recovery expenses for him.

Jesus asked, "Which of the three was a neighbor" to the victim?
The answer, "The man who had mercy on him."
Jesus said, "Go and do likewise." – to any in agony.
Have mercy on your neighbor, friend, stranger, or enemy.

"Love your neighbor as yourself," the moral end:
Love and help those you know, a neighbor or a friend.
Love and help strangers you don't know at your gate.
Love, help and forgive enemies you've learned to hate.

THE TEST–ABRAHAM

In the Old Testament God spoke thru Moses –
The ten commandments laid down the law, no supposes.
The first commandment, number one on the list.
The most important message Jesus said, "it can't be missed."

"Love the Lord your God with all your heart and soul,"
A loving, but jealous God foretold.
God demands man have no other idols before Him.
Love and worship Him only first to escape your sin.

"Love others as you love yourself" – the 2nd commandment,
A lesser priority made clear by God's testament.
We cherish our children whom we totally adore,
But God commands we love Him more.

A child is a beautiful gift from the Lord.
To forfeit a son, a father cannot afford.
It is unnatural for a child to die
Before a parent, causing a compassionate copious cry.

If God told you to sacrifice and kill your only beloved son
To prove your complete obedience to Him, the Holy One –
Could you cut your child's throat and burn him on an altar,
Or would you disobey the Father and falter?

God promised Abraham (95) a son in his old age,
Then gave him Isaac, a miracle heir and sage.
Abraham loved Isaac with absolute appreciation
Whom God pledged to be the leader of the Jewish nation.

Abraham was a successful wealthy man
Tho' the test: to take Abraham's son from him was God's plan.
To prove his love and obedience to God, the Father –
God told Abraham to sacrifice Isaac on the altar.

Abraham idolized Isaac as a perfect son,
But he also loved and honored God, the Holy One.
How could a loyal, loving father choose
His only son to be sacrificed and lose?

Abraham took young Isaac on a journey of several days
A long woeful funeral procession in many ways.
On Mt. Moriah Abraham built an altar of wood,
And prepared the offering as he should.

Abraham took two servants to the foot of Mt. Moriah track –
Told them to wait, while we worship, and **we** will be back.
His faith and trust in God was paramount to his dread –
He probably reasoned God would raise Isaac from the dead.

Isaac asked Abraham where the sacrificial lamb would come from.
Abraham answered, "God will provide the burnt offering, my son."
Abraham bound his son, and held up the knife.
Feel the emotions of Abraham, the worst moment of his life.

How could a father murder his only son today
To satisfy God, the Holy One, and obey?
Abraham must choose between the gift and the giver,
His hands and heart were all a quiver.
His mind was full of doubt –
His promise to God, he wanted out!

Then a voice from Heaven above finally spoke with joy,
"Do not lay a hand on the boy."
"Do not do anything to him," I plea.
"You have not withheld your son from me!"

The first commandment was satisfied at best.
Abraham, tried by God, passed the test.
No other idols before God, His lordship –
Even the idolatry of a beloved child we worship.

Who is primary and your first love –
Spouse, family, friends, or God above?
Will you sacrifice and deny worldly pleasures
For the Creator's eternal given treasures?

If Heaven's gate you want to enter,
The right answers are God and yes, or be a sinner.
Idolatry before God is a sin –
Avoid it with daily discipline!
Trust God first and win!

JOB – THE BET

Job was a righteous man, blameless and upright.
He rejected evil and worshipped God with all his moral might.
Job had many servants, 10 children and thousands of livestock.
He had it all: a rich fortune and wealthy flock.

Satan, the Angel of Death, made God a bet –
If his riches were destroyed, Job would curse God's safety net.
Satan thought Job loved God **only** for the good stuff God gave him.
God believed Job's faith and trust in Him would continue to win.

Then Job had a bad day:
All his servants and farm animals passed away;
They were stolen, burned, killed or elapsed;
And all of Job's children died when a house collapsed.

Job cried, shaved his beard, endured extreme remorse.
He suffered tragedy and pain from the dark source.
He was a living corpse, of course.
But Job refused to curse God, and did affirm,
"Naked I came from my mother's womb, and naked I will return."

Then the bet grew stronger. Satan harmed Job personally.
Sores and boils, head to toe, covered his body totally.
Job scraped his sores with broken pottery and sat in ashes,
But he could not relieve the painful throbbing ravages.

Job's wife told him to curse God and die.
But he replied, "we must accept good **and** evil for God to sanctify."
Job's friends told him he must have committed a horrible sin
To deserve God's severest punishment, the maxim.

Job again refused to curse God for Heaven's sake.
He argued to God, "I am free of sin and deserve a break,"

He accused God of making a mistake.
Since Job was ignorant of God's complicated creation of the Earthly Kingdom,
He was unworthy to question the Almighty's infinite wisdom.

Job's faith in God did never dim.
Finally he said, "Even if He should kill me, I still will trust Him."
Job repented. God restored all the riches Satan had disbursed.
The Lord blessed the last days of Job's life more than the first.

Satan lost the faithful Job bet.
His evil pride will never forget.
Don't ever bet against God, you'll lose.
For the omniscient Lord controls all the realities we choose.

Life is complicated. There are always unanswered questions.
Tragedy and misery always exist for good Christians.
The real question is: not **why** the righteous **endure** suffering,
But **how** the righteous **respond** unwavering.

If man acts right **only** to be rewarded on Earth, it is a no-no,
And righteousness is a poor show that will not grow.
If man abandons his faith because of hardship, then righteousness is worth ZERO.
We cannot comprehend God's infinite wisdom, and never will.
Only faith and trust in Him our hearts fulfill.

God is THE MAN
With THE PLAN
Our LIFESPAN
Will never UNDERSTAND!

THE SOIL SEED SOWER
A PARABLE OF JESUS

A farmer sows seed on four different types of sod.
In Jesus' parable, "seed" signifies "the word of God."
Four types of soil indicate what varied hearts have heard,
The reception and perception of man toward God and His word.

One seed falls on a hardened path, how absurd,
And is immediately eaten by a flock of birds.
This seed means people with a rigid heart toward God's word –
Allow satan to steal their belief so they do not remain saved and preferred.

The second seed falls on rocky soil,
No moisture and no root, the plants wither and spoil.
Some people initially accept God's word faithfully,
But when truth begins to hurt, they abandon Him regretfully.

The third seed falls among thorns and weeds,
Which grow, spread, choke plants and impede.
Man's worries, riches and pleasures supercede,
And the garden of his heart does not mature to lead.

The fourth seed falls on rich productive Earth.
Man receives this seed and enjoys faithful rebirth.
His heart cultivates the fruit of a good life.
Accept His word, retain it, persevere, you'll produce a crop void of strife.

Jesus said, "Though seeing they do not see, hear but do not understand."
Some people don't acquire the truth of sowing seeds for the promised land.
These people will drown in dark eternal quicksand.
Jesus' words weed out thorns, rock, and unclean dirt, a helping hand.

DON'T WORRY
A PARABLE OF JESUS

Jesus said don't worry
About your life.
What you eat or wear,
Life is more than food,
Body more than clothes.
Ravens do not reap nor sow.
No storeroom, nor barn,
Yet God feeds them.
You're more valuable than birds,
Worrying adds not a single hour to life.

"You of little faith!"
Grass grows and wild flowers dress delicate.
Don't worry about food or drink,
Nor clothes you wear.
Your Father knows you need them,
Seek His Kingdom.
These things will be given to you.
Sell your possessions,
Give to the poor,
Where your treasure is,
There will be your heart also.

THE WICKED TENANTS
Jesus Parable – Matthew 21:33 – 46

A landowner planted a vineyard,
Built a stonewall around it,
Rented it to tenant-farmers,
And moved to another place.
At harvest time, he sent servants
To collect the fruits.
The tenants, beat, stoned and killed the servants.
More servants sent were also killed.
The landowner sent his son, his cornerstone,
Thinking the tenants would respect him.
But the greedy tenants also killed the son
To seize his inheritance.
Jesus asked what will the landowner do?
The Jewish Priests in the temple answered,
Kill the tenants, and rent the vineyard
To other farmers, who will harvest the crops.

Then Jesus said,
The Kingdom of God will be taken from you,
And given to a people who will produce righteous fruit,
Meaning the New Church.
The landowner was God.
The vineyard was the Kingdom of God.
Jesus was the Divine Son, the cornerstone,
Fulfilling the death prophecy.
Anyone who kills and rejects the Stone
Will be crushed.
The servants were emissaries of God –
John the Baptist and Jesus,
Who were beaten and killed
By the Jewish leaders,
Thus undermining Jesus' authority.

The priests feared
Jesus' popularity with the crowds,
Knew He was talking about them,
And had pronounced their own judgment.

THE MARRIAGE FEAST
Jesus Parable – Luke 14:15; Matthew 22:1-14

A King prepared a marriage feast for his son
With fattened cattle, cooked and ready.
Twice his servants invited guests,
Who refused to come.
Excuses: business; attend fields; just married.
Some invitees killed the King's servants.
The King was angry,
Sent his army to destroy them,
Burned the city.
The King said – go to highways and street corners,
Invite others: good and bad,
Lame, poor, crippled and blind.
Some still refused to come.
One man came, not attired
In proper wedding clothes,
The King threw him out.

The marriage feast represents the Father,
Christ, and Kingdom of God.
Blessed are those who eat at the banquet.
Refusal to attend
Shows disloyalty and discourtesy.
Burned the city is destruction of Jerusalem.
The day will come,
When God no longer invites
Those who repeatedly refuse Him.
Invitations to others – gentiles, etc.,
Come only on God's terms.
Man is responsible for his
Indifference and self-righteousness.
The man with no wedding clothes
Claims to be ready for God's Kingdom,

But is not.
Good and bad are invited,
But few are chosen.

THE PEARL
Jesus Parable – Matthew 13:44-46

The Kingdom of Heaven,
Like treasure
Hidden in a field.
A man found it,
Sold all he had,
Bought the field.

The Kingdom of Heaven,
Like fine pearls.
A merchant found
One of great value,
Sold everything he had,
And bought it.

The merchant-man
Is Christ,
Seeking good men and women,
Fine pearls,
Who respond to His message.
Christ gave all He had –
His Life –
To create the New Church.

THE NET
Jesus Parable – Matthew 13:47-52

The Kingdom of Heaven,
Like a net
Cast into the sea,
Caught all kinds of fish.
Fishermen kept good fish
In a basket,
And bad fish
Thrown away.

The net is the gospel.
The sea is all nations.
Jesus interpreted –
Good fish are responsive to gospel.
Bad fish are wicked men
Put in the net by Satan.

RICH FOOL
A JESUS PARABLE

A rich man yielded
An abundant harvest.
I have no place
To store all my crops.
I will tear down all my barns,
Build bigger barns.
I'll have plenty of grain,
Laid up for many years.
I'll rest, take life easy,
Drink and be merry.

God said, "You Fool!"
This very night
Your life will flicker out.
Then who will inherit
What you stashed for yourself?
Watch out for greed.
Life is not hording self-possessions,
But laying away treasures
In your heart
Rich toward God.

THE RAPTURE

The Rapture, an Awesome Awakening –
Jesus is coming, Jesus is coming
For the second time,
Superb and sublime,
Offering His lifeline
For eternal sunshine.

The Rapture, "Blessed Hope and Confidence" –
Jesus shouts from the air His Holy guidance:
All believers; innocent children; and sleepers rise from the grave;
Rapture to Heaven with Him, who forgave;
Resurrected souls to save.

When will Jesus come? Soon!
Don't know when, but anytime now, I assume!
Are you always rapture ready?
Is your faith in the Son of God steady?

Believers need not worry about the tribulation,
They'll live forevermore in Heaven's reincarnation.
"Thank you Lord, for rescuing an imperfect sinful creature,
Allowing me to enjoy your snatching rapture."
Obey and trust Jesus in you heart and mind,
You will not be left behind.

END TIMES PROPHECY
Future Biblical Sequence

THE RAPTURE
Suddenly, "The Blessed Hope" with no forewarning,
A rapture or snatching of millions upbringing.
Jesus Christ calls from the air
All the believers in Him who care.

Some of our family and friendly lovers
Will not arise from under the covers.
Ones who have not found Christ
Not lifted to paradise.

Jesus' Bride, the gentile church; all believers!
The dead, live ones, innocent children, heavenly receivers;
Even individual Jews who accept Christ and believe.
But the Israel Nation, which rejected Jesus on the cross, will not receive.

Jesus guides His faithful flock
To His Father in Heaven in peaceful arm lock.
Righteous transformed bodies transported to God's house.
To live forever in His kingdom as a loving spouse.

THE TRIBULATION
The unraptured unbelievers, Jesus-blind
Left on Earth behind
To suffer for 7 years
"The wrath of God," tribulation tears.

Armageddon, apocalypse, world at war,
Horrific devastation, planet Earth tore, an eyesore.
Vegetation, air, oceans, fresh waters polluted,
Millions of believers and unbelievers executed.

Earthquakes, volcanic, cosmic disruption,
Armies killing, nuclear weapons of mass destruction,
Demonic locust plagues attacking from the bottomless pit,
Sun, moon, stars spiraling out of orbit.

"The Antichrist," Satan, false prophets worldwide rule,
During the tribulation 7 year evil demonic schedule.
"The Beast" dictates the sign of 666,
A permanent mark on all human foreheads or wrists to fix.

Prove loyalty to "the antichrist's" hysterics.
Without the mark: can't buy or sell the basics.
If you reject the sign on your body,
Judgment: starve, or head cut off to disembody.

Tribulation purpose: give unbelievers and Jewish Nation a 2nd chance
To repent, accept Jesus as the Messiah, and advance,
Pardoned to the Father's heavenly kingdom
To fulfill God's promise of Israel's fee simple fiefdom.

During the tribulation all unbelievers will be saved,
If they accept the Lord, and are believer brave.
For "the antichrist" will condemn their courage and His distrust,
Cut off their heads in unjust blood lust.

THE MILLENIUM
At the end of the tribulation,
Jesus' physical 2nd coming to Earth in jubilation,
Riding a white horse, His "glorious appearing"
To destroy "the antichrist" armies, disappearing.

Jesus achieves victory over Satan's 7 tribulation years,
Installs the 1,000 year millennium with holy cheers.
Jesus promised, "I will come again."
To repopulate the Earth with righteous men.

At the end of the 1,000 year millennium
Satan released from prison to again tempt pandemonium,
Evil free choice to reject Christ and go to hell.
Those who call the name of the Lord, saved, and in Heaven dwell.

When is the final end of Earth time?
Not explained in the Bible, nor this simple rhyme.

SUMMIT SUMMARY

Two thousand years ago
The Bible tells us so.
In Bethlehem, an ancient land –
A virgin child, born by predestined plan:
Jesus grew into a perfect man –
God's Son, "The Christ," began.
Through His words and miracle deeds –
He challenged the Jews indeed.
He was nailed to the cross by the conspiring Jews,
Who were threatened by His gospel news.
He could have saved himself from death,
But He chose freely His dying breath.
His doom was the point of a perfect end –
For His sacrifice freed us from all our sin.
But the story does not stop here –
Three days later, cried the Christian cheer:
Jesus revived and lived again –
So that now all who believe in Him,
And accept Him into their hearts –
Will never die and enjoy eternal starts.

PERSONAL BELIEFS

MY HUMBLE DAILY PRAYER

Dear God I love you as a son loves a father –
Dear Jesus I love you as a brother loves a brother –
Absolutely and unconditionally –
Until the end of eternity.

God I believe you sent Jesus to Earth (1) as an example
Of a perfect human being without sin;
(2) And to teach mankind **how to live without sin, and**

(3) God I believe you also sent your Son to be sacrificed
On the cross to save us all from all our sins –
If we only believe . . . and repent of all our sins, and follow Jesus' teachings.
And dear God – I believe in your Son and repent with all
My heart and soul; and try to follow in your Son's footsteps!

God forgive me for all of my sins, which I commit against you every day,
And grant me eternal life with you
And your Son, Jesus, in Heaven for the
Rest of time!
I believe in your Son, Jesus: His
Virgin birth, His crucifixion, His
Resurrection, His rapture,
His ascension into Heaven, and His
Second coming, when He will be called
The King of Kings and the Lord of Lords!

Jesus, I believe in you and I receive you!
I also pray for my intimate family, several families,
Approximately 50 people by name, who I love and care for:
That they receive inner peace, good health, and
That you heal them spiritually, physically and mentally.
And if any of them have cancer – please rid them of their
Cancer, and keep it out of their bodies.

I pray to you, God: I love, worship, thank, praise,
Trust, depend on you and need you – to live in my heart. I Pray that you
Protect me from the evil one, and guide me to do
What's right and righteous; do unto others as I would have them
Do unto me, and love others as I love myself, and help me to resist sin, and
Guide me to achieve my God given purposes on Earth.

I pray in your name, dear God, and for the
Glorification of your Son, Jesus Christ. Amen!

THANKSGIVING DAY PRAYER

Lord, bless all of us,
And this food!
Thank you Jesus,
As we believe in you renewed!

CHRISTMAS CRUNCH

Christmas commercials in mid November,
Avoiding the rush in late December.
Early decorations hanging all around,
Holiday parades in every town.

Traditional Christmas T.V. shows:
Frosty and Rudolph with the red nose;
The Grinch and Scrooge, powerful examples;
Substitute Santas selling samples.

Mailing Christmas cards to forgotten friends,
Stretching the budget beyond its ends.
Worrying if the gift you selected,
Is right for the one you projected.

Choosing the perfect Christmas tree.
Its O.K. for you, but what about me?
Too skinny, too short without the best crown?
No matter—the children will pull it down!

Scurrying about in a panic, trying to shop;
The gift list never seems to stop.
Standing in lines gets weary and old,
Then you discover it's already been sold.

Mail out-of-town packages early to avoid the stew,
Forget a gift for one who remembers you.
Wrapping packages and cooking all day;
Order toys now, worry later how you will pay.

Office and club parties do abound -
With the same people and boring sound.
Too much rich food and flowing booze -
Hangovers and indigestion, it's hard to snooze.

Cleaning the house to decorate.
Trim the tree; get mad at your mate.
Referee the excited children's fights;
Work feverishly and stay up nights.

The hectic pace is always fast,
No different from years gone past.
'Tis finally Christmas eve.
The silent stillness hard to believe.

Relax again and meditate –
The physical and mental pressures now abate.
But the real reason for it all makes it great –
For it's Christ's Birthday we celebrate.

TRILOGY ANALOGY

Christ is in God.
God is in Christ.
The Holy Spirit is in Christ.
Christ is in the Holy Spirit.
God is in the Holy Spirit.
The Holy Spirit is in God.
The Holy Trilogy we agree:
One saint all three.

I am in God.
God is in me.
I am in Christ.
Christ is in me.
I am in the Holy Spirit.
The Holy Spirit is in me.
I am a saint by analogy.
Could it be? Not likely!

THE CALENDAR

All the world relies on the yearly standard today.
What is the reference to convey?
Our calendars recite the year 2015, we say
The birthdate of Jesus does portray
All the markings of time, I pray,
Relate to before or after Jesus' Birthday.

Our measure of total time, we conceive
Proof that in Jesus, we all must believe.

TRUTH

Where is inherent truth?
Within the burden of proof?

Let's take a look:
Find it in a book?
The author knows it all –
Not that I recall!

Is it on the witness stand –
Not in this great land!
Is it a complicated mystery –
Hidden deep in history?

Does philosophy hold the answer,
Or maybe the graceful gypsy dancer?
Is it cosmopolitan charm,
Or life on a tranquil farm?

Is it knowledge –
Learned in college?
Or experience practiced on the streets –
Taught by many seasoned feats?

Does it emerge from a flower bloom,
Or born from the mother's womb?
Does it migrate with the geese flying South,
Or speak from the innocent children's mouth?

Who knows where it lies –
Far up there in the skies?
Deep down in the earth below,
Or nestled in the new born snow?

Is it encircled in the joyful smile,
Or stacked in a golden pile?
Is it latently ecumenical,
Or concealed by a mercenary criminal?

Search for it in the clover –
Look everywhere and all over.
Seek it out in the art,
Begin again at the start.

Truth is what we perceive.
What we honestly believe.
Sincere faith is truth.
Found in eternal youth.

Is it hiding from all the sinners,
Or waiting for the wanting winners?
Is it from the hymnals sung,
Or praised by the preachers' tongue?

Who knows –
Where truth grows?
In this prose –
No one knows!

THE DOOR

There are different types of doors
We walk thru to upper floors.
There is a literal door not a metaphor,
Built from wood and stone to explore,
And figurative doors we conceive
Formed from faith and images we believe.

The "Judge is at the door," a figure of speech
Not a literal door, but a parable to teach
An allusion to the final portal,
When you near the end of mortal.
"The Judge" will arbitrate the wicked and righteous –
Will you be a sinner or saintly pious?
When the judgment gate swings open,
Will your actions be Christ-like or broken?

Be a believer and receiver of God and His Son,
And pass thru the entrance door to Kingdom Come!

A PRAYER FOR HELP

We pray to God for a favor.
His wisdom we savor.
He may not answer today,
He will in His own way.
We are pawns in His hand.
He directs us to the promised land.
Have patience as He leads
Us to our desired needs.
It may not be exactly what we ask,
Faith in Him endures the task.
Remind Him everyday,
Be assured it'll be His own way.
Peaceful patience guides us,
If in Him we place our total trust.

FORGIVENESS

We pray God will forgive
All those sins we live.
You're confident He will answer this prayer,
But be wary of this snare:
If we don't excuse others first
God will not quinch our thirst.
Initiate the pardon of others with serious care,
Only then will God return your humble prayer.
Don't be bitter, nor hate –
So God will forgive you and reciprocate.

REPENTANCE

"Lord, I'm really sorry I sinned.
I certainly hope I never do it again."
"Lord, I'm really sorry I got caught."
Is this genuine repentance? Naught!

"Lord, you know I'm human and not perfect.
Another made me make my mistake incorrect."
Blaming others for our sin
Is not complete repentance within.

When we sin, we hurt others.
But our sin is not against our brothers.
We sin only against God, not our fellow man.
Our weaknesses and failures are God's sole plan.

Our sins we attempt to cover up –
This is dishonest and corrupt.
When we confess our incorrigibility –
We must take full responsibility.

Deal with your sin genuinely and openly.
Don't delay, be wise, repent hurriedly.
God will lessen the severity of your discipline today,
If you immediately correct your sin and obey!

Repentance and belief in the resurrected Lord
Are the same and of one accord.
Without both you need not bother –
You cannot have one without the other.

Genuine repentance is not coerced –
Receive and believe in Christ first.
Repent sincerely and change your wicked behavior –
Faith in Christ – receive Him as your personal savior.

LOVE

Love, the word, is not the issue.
Love is not a simple, "I Love You!"
Love from the soul is the only virtue.
Love is not what you pursue, but what you do.
Love from the spirit makes it true.
Love is what your heart will do.

Good food is not delicious until you eat it.
An athletic contest is not fulfilling until you win it.
An education is not satisfying until you earn it.
Hard work is not enjoyed until you finish it.
Youth is not gratifying until you miss it.
Love is not contentment until you give it.

True love is a sure gateway.
Faithful love will not betray.
Pure love is like Mother's Day.
Enjoy eternal love and pray.
Love is not what you say.
Love is what you give away.

SUICIDE

Suicide: killing oneself, an intentional act.
It is wrong and a sin in fact.
Rebellion against God is intended.
Only God decides when your life is ended.

Suicide: motivated by a cause or pact;
Feelings of depression and meaningless life exact;
Extended illness and unbearable pain;
Inability to cope with failure and relationships came.

Suicide: self-hatred, a lack of faith, and
It usurps God's power and preordained plan.
"Love our neighbors as ourselves" – one holy command.
Life is God's gift – not our decision to demand.

You're separated from God when you rebel.
If you don't believe in Christ, your destiny is hell.
But those who accept Christ will always belong.
There is no condemnation for this final wrong.

God's promise to all who honor the resurrected Christ above
Will forever have God's mercy and everlasting love.
For God's grace and promise is eternally endured,
And absolute forgiveness is heavenly assured.

Is suicide a pardonable sin?
Will this final self-murder be forgiven?
For those in Christ Jesus who self-kill –
Does God forgive their suicide? Yes, He will!

Footnote:
The Bible declares only one unpardonable (blasphemy) sin –
Attributed to the Pharisees way back when.
They said Jesus' miracles came from Satan's force,
When in fact The Holy Spirit was the true source.

FORBIDDEN SEX

If man has sex with a man,
And woman has sex with a woman –
Is this a detestable, unpardonable sin
That denies Heaven to enter in?

God, thru Moses in the Old Testament Plan
Warns man not to have sex with a man
As one does with a woman –
This is detestable and punished by death's hand

However, Moses does not warn women to refrain
From having sex with other women to blame.
The ancient Jews apparently could not conceive
Two women engaging in same sex, I believe.

If you are lesbian or homosexual brethren,
Are you sure to reside with God in Heaven?
Confirm your ultimate pardon so in hell you do not roam –
If you continue to be uncertain of your eternal home.

Let our Lord know where your true heart stands
So your sinful spirit soars into His comforting hands.
Pray forgiveness of all your sins with your last breath,
Or write a letter asking forgiveness to be published at your death.

Jesus' words in the New Testament reveal
Nothing about this forbidden sex appeal –
Between man and man,
Nor between woman and woman.

Jesus forgives all wicked sinners.
Those who love and seek Him are all winners.
If all sinners beg forgiveness to Him,
They will be granted entry into Heaven – Amen!

God has mercy on all human beings,
And expects us to show others mercy feelings.
God's grace grants mercy for us to be forgiven,
And mercy trumps over judgment sin.

Be merciful to all others.
Love them like long lost brothers.
Good and bad people are God's creation.
Love all people equally to avoid temptation.

The 2nd Commandment, "The Royal Law," itself;
"Love your neighbor as yourself."
Do not seek revenge or bear a grudge
Against your people – be a gracious judge.

What is hateful to you –
To your neighbor, do not do!
The righteous life God requires of you –
Show your good Samaritan love to be true!

Love your neighbor, a person of needs.
Respect that person, do courteous deeds.
I have done God's will,
When I love others as myself to fulfill.

Who are we to judge others –
Our odd and deviate sisters and brothers?
If they seek goodwill and are just –
They create a better world of solidarity, I trust.

He who is without sin alone –
Let him cast the first stone.
If a gay person seeks the Lord –
Why should we throw the first sword?

Having sex among the same gender,
Is apparently true love very tender.
If loving consenting parties agree,
We may not understand their harmony.

But why should this offend you and me?
Let God judge their hearts to see,
If they've accepted Christ and repented to The Holy Trinity,
He is the ultimate judge, let them be!

BEGIN AGAIN

We pray our sinful stupid ways
Be hurled on rocky shores as castaways,
Donated like worn out clothes to goodwill,
Never seen again their end fulfill.
We've all made miserable mistakes on this Earth.
Thru Christ's forgiving rebirth
We will live in Heaven –
Begin again! Amen!

FAITH - BELIEVE!

We don't know what we don't know,
Then how can we believe it so?
A will to believe, or a will not to believe -
Faith is a choice only the Loving Heart can perceive.

True knowledge is a fact supreme.
Faith is the evidence of things unseen.
If I tell you I have a diamond in my closed hand -
You can't see it, but believe it thru faith, you understand.

Belief and doubt can co-exist -
Only the dark heart will try to resist.
Faith challenged by adversity is strongest in the end.
Realistic faith trusts God in healing or in death, Amen!

I believe, but will you help me with my unbelief?
It's hard to believe when loved ones suffer grief.
Where is God you cry and pray -
Why won't He heal my dearly beloved today?

Jesus says, all things are possible to those who believe.
But God resolves the problem in a way only He can conceive -
We may not understand His exact reply -
All we can do is wonder why,
And know His solution will rectify.

Some people choose not to believe and have no faith.
All unbelief has other underlying reasons to be unsafe.
If you follow and learn from Jesus, who you respect,
You will commit to faith in God and be at peace perfect.
Even if you have some doubts, you can choose belief,
And seek God to help you with your unbelief.

FAN OR FOLLOWER?

A fan believes in Jesus with his mind.
A follower engages his total heart to Jesus in kind.
Are you an enthusiastic admiring Jesus fan?
Or 100% committed to follow the Jesus plan?

God loved the world (and His people) so much
He sacrificed His only begotten Son to touch
So those who believe in His identity
Will not perish, but live forever in infinity.
JOHN 3:16

If we merely believe in Jesus, it's so simple –
We will live forever in God's holy temple.
God promises us eternal life as a fan,
But there is more commitment to His heavenly plan.

If anyone comes after God's pleasures –
He must deny himself earthly treasures,
And take up His cross daily,
And follow God, the master, gaily.
LUKE 9:23

Everyone who loses his life for Jesus will save it.
Surrender your freedoms to the Holy Spirit.
Imitate Jesus exclusively – no exceptions.
Be a slave to God – just say no to your imperfections.

Say no to self – yes to Jesus every time.
No reserves, no regrets, no retreats – no mine.
Come and die to your own evil desires.
Seek Jesus daily – put out the unholy fires.

Follow after Jesus – deny alcohol, drugs and porn.
Deny yourself – over family, career goals and coin.
Don't worry about what other people think.
Be a slave to God – avoid idolatry gods, or sink.

GRACE

Evildoers live life immoral and impure,
Mercy and kindness eternally endure.
"Amazing grace" is perfect and pure,
Healing sinners with compassionate cure.

Not thru our good works will our souls uplift –
We are saved only thru faith by God's gift.
We are all sinners and deserve condemnation –
But thru God's grace alone we come to salvation.

Don't boast of all the good you've done.
Only God provides sinners' needs thru His Son.
God loves us not for what we've done, or will do.
Our full sin-debt was paid on the cross, His I.O.U.

Thru grace we serve Him
Because we love Him
Not to earn His favor,
But to receive Christ our Saviour.

God's grace accepts us on another's merits –
Not thru our deeds, but thru acts of the Holy Spirit.
During our suffering – grace is strong in our weakness.
Grace super-abounds our pain in His loving kindness.

Thru Jesus Christ came grace and truth.
2000 years ago life was cheap, and there is proof:
Evil empires conquered nations with military might –
They killed and controlled mankind with fearful terrifying fright.

Only the strong survived, not the weak.
Then Christ said, "Love your enemies; turn the other cheek" –
Christianity won over the evil military force –
By changing hearts and minds from within of course.

The power of the Christian message spread worldwide,
Empowering man to overcome evil magnified.
The human race was impacted with grace and good –
Thru the influence of God's grace as it should.

Grace serves all mankind thru God's promises
Of kindness, forgiveness, integrity and services.
A father warns his children of dangers with tough love –
Like God, a stern judge, mercifully rules from above.

The impact of God's "Amazing Grace"
Reveals to us the true value of the Human Race:
The grace effect gives us the dignity of a human life;
Protection of children; and women's strife;

The abolition of slavery; charitable giving;
Caring for the poor, sick, weak, starving and living;
Ethnic equality; liberty and freedom.
The touch of grace lights up God's Earthly Kingdom.

We are all sinners and do not deserve Heaven.
Our sins of pride, selfishness, lust and rebellion should not be forgiven.
Only God's gift of salvation thru His grace,
And Christ's death and resurrection we embrace,
Will allow us to enter God's Holy Place.

WHEN HARM HAPPENS TO HARMLESS HUMANS
OR
WHEN INJURY/ILLNESS INFLICTS INNOCENT INDIVIDUALS
OR
WHEN BAD THINGS HAPPEN TO GOOD PEOPLE

Tragedy smashes you in the face stunned,
Or seizes your loved one –
Paralyzed by an auto accident done –
Cancer or terminal illness begun.

You believe you are good as a nun,
A righteous, upright and moral son.
You worship and follow Jesus well-done.
Pray God will grant you a pardon.

You pray for a medical miracle to be done.
Remember: God denied a life saving miracle for His only Son.
But then He restored His Son's life as The Holy One.
God can't grant the exception to the rule for everyone.

God doesn't pass out miracles like Halloween candy.
We shouldn't expect them so easy and handy.
God hears millions of praying petitions,
If He granted them all, no need for doctors or morticians.

Does God punish good people with bad things?
No! He cares and weeps for you, and has only love feelings.
For the humans He created,
He does not want us incapacitated!

Believe and have faith in God's goodness and fairness,
Even if you've been hurt by life's madness.
Misery happens to good and bad people equally.
Evil random attacks occur to all of us regretfully.

God does not test or punish us for our sin.
His ultimate goal for us is to begin again and win.
God loves us and is on our side -
Turn to Him for strength and be glorified.

Why does God let bad things happen to good people,
Causing them pain, suffering, or being a cripple?
The explanation is: He cannot control it all!
Can God divert disaster after the fact? Not that I recall!

You ask - isn't God omniscient and omnipotent in fact,
All-seeing, all-knowing, all-powerful before the tragedy act?
There are reasons God will not intervene -
One is: He gave man moral freedom to be mean.

Since the beginning in the Garden of Eden we understood -
God gave man free will to choose evil or good.
Man can drive an automobile drunk, or be sober as he should
To avoid a fatal wreck, if he would,
Or choose not to intentionally murder like a mafia hood.

Some terminal illnesses are not man-made,
But caused by genes, bad luck, or germs that invade.
God has other limitations; restricted by the impossible and natural laws.
Bad stuff happens at times with no reasoned cause.

Don't ask: why did this tragedy happen to me? - How?
Ask: what do I do now?
All our families experience sad sorrow.
The real question is: How can I heal and grow tomorrow?

No pain, no gain.
Crisis creates character, not shame.
Trust, obey God and His reasons -
Altho unknown to us - they can be good conclusions.

God grows good from tragic situations.
We cozy closer to Him and others thru restorations.
Out of chaos He produces strength, courage and hope
So that innocent victims of bad things can cope.

Believe in God, He is not arbitrary, but fair.
His final solution will be filled with loving grace and care.
Through the fire of suffering God will be just.
Rely on His strength, not your own, in His trust.

God, himself, suffered bad things, the ultimate loss,
When His perfect Son died on the cross.
His extreme pain proved His sacrificial love for us.
Therefore, we can relate to His tragedy thru His Son Jesus.

Bad stuff happens in life, get over it!
Temporary pain on Earth tests our limit.
In Heaven all pain you will *forgit*.
Look forward to God's eternity for glorious benefit.

Life is painfully hard.
Temporary suffering on Earth, disregard.
God is our lifeguard.
Heaven is our credit card.

God is THE MAN
With THE PLAN
Our LIFESPAN
Will never UNDERSTAND!

Christ Believers are at war with the devil.
Satan deceives and manipulates us with demonic evil.
SATAN, NOT GOD, CAUSES BAD THINGS TO OPPRESS GOOD PEOPLE.
God heals us through His Son's sacrificial example. ^{ACTS 10:38}

THE TICKET TO HEAVEN

The funeral preacher said: "The dearly departed deceased
Has gone to a better place, to Heaven he's released."
We hope and assume this is true,
But it only applies to a faithful few.
Some sinners, who reject Jesus,
Go to Hell, Believe us!

Being a good person on Earth
Does not guarantee Heaven's rebirth.
Good is not good enough,
If you don't have faith in the Jesus stuff.
Good works are not the certain causation,
But the result of spiritual salvation.

We have all sinned and fall short of God's promised land.
If we break just one of His Laws - in hell we will stand.
Whoever keeps the whole law, and yet stumbles a little bit
Is guilty of breaking all of it.
If we lie once, steal one thing, have one lustful thought, any vice,
We will not enter God's paradise.

God does not overlook, nor tolerate sin.
Any minor transgression can't exist in God's presence to win.
God, a judge, is kind, fair, patient, and forgiving,
But if you reject Him and His Son, there is no thanksgiving -
He will punish sacrilegious hypocrites, if they ignore Him,
And they will enter eternal damnation in ultimate grim.

If a stranger knocks at your door;
You don't know him, and you will ignore;
And not let him in your house without friendly companionship.
God is the same - with no intimate relationship,
He will ignore your knock, and turn you away.
But if you love and experience Him, then you can enter today and stay.

God sent His only Son, perfect without sin
To die, shed His blood on the cross, and rise again
To save us all from our sin – debt;
So when we die, we survive in His eternal safety net.
But we must have faith and accept His Son,
And repent of all our sins to be redone!

This is the only ticket to Heaven, don't delay!
It is a one-way invitation to paradise to forever stay.
Beg for and punch your admission ticket today.
Get down on your knees now, sincerely believe in Jesus and pray!
Then He will forever hug you to His bosom, and never let you stray.
He will eternally love and guide you, the Bible does say.

KEYS TO THE KINGDOM

The greatest moral philosopher ever in fact
Was Jesus Christ whose teachings existed exact.
His lessons and parables for us He intended
Not only to consider, but be acted upon extended.
Hear His words, but not do them, you'll be banned –
Like a foolish man who builds his house on soft sand.

If someone strikes you, be meek –
Turn the other cheek.
Love your enemies with a smile –
Forgive them, go the extra mile.

Do to others what you want them to you to do –
Love others as you self-love you.
Worship only Jesus as a perfect brother –
Do heartfelt kindness to another.

Jesus delivered His Sermon on the Mount –
The Beatitudes or Blessings by Biblical account:

Blessed are the poor –
For they are what Heaven is for.

Blessed are those who mourn –
For they will be comforted and reborn.

Blessed are those who hunger and thirst –
For they shall be filled first.

Blessed are those who are merciful –
For they shall receive mercy so plentiful.

Blessed is the peacemaker –
For he shall be the child of God, the Holy Care Taker.

Do not commit murder.
Don't even remain angry or madder.
Don't think you are superior to others.
Don't call them fools or harbor rage against your brothers.

If we lust after another's body parts –
We've already committed adultery in our hearts.
Don't lie or swear false oaths, be honest so –
Yes means yes, and no means no.

Stop comparing yourself to your neighbor's achievement.
Everyone of us has room for improvement.
When comparing ourselves to God's perfection,
We are a simple inferior defection.

Don't be like an actor on a stage,
Pretending what you are not. Act your age.
Don't practice only self-righteousness for public consumption –
Pious hypocrites pretend to prove a false assumption.

Love the Lord your God at full-length
With all your heart, soul, mind and strength.
If you truly love God and your neighboring brothers,
Then you will obey God and do good to others.

Above are Jesus' Keys to unlock the Heavenly door –
Your loving heart should attempt to explore.
Apply His words to your actions while you are living –
Then He'll unlock the door to the Kingdom with merciful forgiving.

IT'S NEVER TOO LATE

We are all sinners – the bad news.
Old Testament punishment was death – our just dues.
Then God gave us His Only Son – the good news.
Belief in Jesus equals eternal life – don't refuse.

We know for sure we will die.
We never know when, how or why.
If you've not accepted Christ, is it too late?
It will be your fate, if you procrastinate.

You've lived a long, sinful and wild life.
Should you expect a perfect after life?
No! Unless in Christ you care.
Kneel down now, pray and prepare!

You think God ignores you?
No! He loves and adores you!
He created us all everyone
To gather in Heaven, if you believe in His Son.

It takes only one second to accept Jesus and repent -
For eternal life, time well spent.
Beware! If you delay to the end,
You may unexpectedly die with no time to amend.

Jesus and two thieves being crucified on the cross –
All three suffering at death's door, what a loss.
One thief heard Jesus pray for His killers, forgiving;
And profess self love and protection for His mother, living.

"Remember me when you come to your kingdom," that thief said to Christ.
Jesus replied, "Today you will be with me in paradise."
It wasn't too late for that thief to act.
Jesus proved: "it's never too late" for Heaven in fact.

GOOD -v- EVIL

Good and Evil in the world are real and exist.
You cannot know one without the other, I insist.
Compare wrong to right,
Like day to night.

Opposites are different and contrast.
You're not aware of one without the last.
You don't appreciate cold unless you've been hot,
A straight line is crooked – not.

Some humans are greedy, malicious, wicked and evil;
Devil-like, deceitful, immoral, vicious people.
Some are saints, not sinners, worthy and do good;
Angelic, innocent, virtuous and act as they should.

Did God create evil? No!
He made moral laws for us to follow and know.
He gave us free choice
To choose right or wrong thru his voice.

God could have made us robots to obey Him blindly
That would not have served us kindly.
With free choice He also warned of dangers we would endure
Thru Biblical gospels and Ten Commandments so pure.

With God we learn to save, protect ourselves and others,
To live good and righteous lives as peaceful loving brothers.
If we follow His teachings and moral laws,
We avoid the devil's evil jaws.

What would the world be like with no God today?
Evil would be permissible to guide our lives in a bad way.
"Do evil to others before they do it to you" –
Would be the wrong golden rule to adhere to.

Why is there evil in the human race?
Should God destroy all evil and put it in its place?
After Noah's flood, God promised never to kill all mankind again.
Only in man's heart dwells evil sin.
Don't kill the body, heal the heart within!

God defines and denounces evil thru His Commandments.
He mercifully warns and protects us from evil with His judgments.
God defeats sin thru His Son's death on the cross.
He absorbs our evil punishment, forgives and saves us from our loss.

Jesus' words in the gospels define our wrongs,
Heals our sinful separation from God and makes us strong.
Evil had a beginning, and it will also have an end.
Free will exists in Heaven with no evil – Amen!

THE ALTERNATIVE

Silent fog creeps over grave stones
Malicious winds rattle cryptic bones.
Fearful darkness generates immortal moans
Decaying flesh invades supernatural homes.

From out of the cold comatose night
Lurks a corpselike chilling fright.
A pale phantom prowls with morbid eyes
No mortal views the monstrous surprise.

Freshly interred specter cannot speak
Grotesque shape mesmerized and weak.
Living dead, cadaverous and insane
Lying in earthen casket with everlasting pain.

Agonizing destiny to roam – perpetually;
Immortally paralyzed in suffering – habitually.
Excommunicated from mankind and human reason
Heinous heathen without heavenly season.

Ghost-like body hanging in suspension,
Hideous features too harsh to mention.
Caught between Heaven and Hell,
Pendulating nowhere in the enchanting spell.

Doomed for eternal damnation
Fear of no hope and no salvation.
The evil human soul postponed too late
Self destruction predetermined its frightful fate.

Where did it come from – where to go?
Beguiling fate of an unfortunate foe.
Only one absolute solution
Repentance from sin with complete absolution.
. . . . Is it too late . . . . ? NO!

THE AFTERLIFE

Have you thought about it?
When you die do you quit?
Do you remain in a casket?
Do you turn to dust in a pit?
Is death dark and unlit?
With family can you visit?
Does your existence forfeit?
Is death only an exit?
I don't know I admit!
But God knows all of it!

Do you live again as a spirit?
Does your body and soul split?
Will your soul rise into orbit?
Were your values unfit, or legit?
Will good deeds of your life be writ?
Were you an evil culprit?
Was your heart decrepit, or have any merit?
Did you live for others benefit?
I don't know I admit!
But God knows all of it!

HEAVEN -v- HELL

When we die, we have three choices:
Nothing, Hell or Heavenly voices.
There are consequences for our worth on Earth.
The decisive destiny is Heaven or Hell for our rebirth.

If we go to sleep and never wake up,
Our life is over and the end is abrupt.
All our Earthly existence would be good for nothing,
Unless there are real purposes for our living.
Therefore, nothing is not an option for believing.

Death is not eternal extinctions:
Heaven and Hell are literal and real dimensions.
All Biblical messages extol:
Humans have a body, spirit and soul.

Our body in the earth will forever lie,
But the soul and spirit will never die.
Our immortal spirits will be conscious after death.
Heaven or Hell is the final destination at our last breath.

Will you reject Christ and enjoy nothing good,
Or Live In Christ, as your endless soul should?
Will you choose perpetual punishment and hell fire,
Or no sickness, no pain, and listen to the heavenly choir?

Will you select utter hopelessness, crushing despair and abysmal loneliness,
Or enjoy Jesus, family and loved ones with no stress?
Will you prefer no friends, darkness, silence and isolation,
Or a mansion, streets of pure gold and peaceful jubilation?

Will you pick horrid smells, no food, no hope, no love,
Or beautiful trees, rivers, mountains and banquets up above?

Will you elect to be with demons and burn in the land of no return,
Or be with angels, joy, forgiveness and peace well-earned?

Will you embrace endless misery and eternal damnation,
Or the perfect place of righteous holy celebration?
Will you decide to be a lost soul forever dead,
Or wrap yourself in lasting, loving warmth instead?

If you seek satan's falsifying, fiery torment,
You'll be trapped in burning flames, hell-bent.
Pray to God and die In Christ,
And live forever in paradise.

Satan's promises are none.
Dump the devil and be done.
Embrace Jesus, The Holy Son.
The choice is an easy one.

A VISION OF HELL

Awake, not a nightmare, nor dream.
Falling, plunging, a long dark tunnel, sense a scream.
Landing hard on stone floor in Hell.
Thick metal bars, no windows, a prison cell.

Dark as a bottomless coal mine, no light.
Pitch black–jailed in eternal night.
No air, only brimstone and smoke.
No oxygen, no breath, evoking choke.

No water, parched lips and throat, dry desert thirst.
No moisture, dehydrated, cursed, the worst.
No rest, no sleep, tired, weary and weak
No strength, total exhaustion, a feeble freak.

No food, no nourishment, no feast, no bread, nor meat.
Void stomach, starving, hungry for a meal, nothing to eat.
Decaying, disgusting, rancid smells, suffocating everyone.
Stinking like sewer, garbage, rotten eggs, skunks, all-in-one.

No love here, only hostile hate.
Non-believing offenders eternal fate.
No trust, no smiles, no joy, no tender affection.
No sympathy, no care for others, mere malicious rejection.

No companionship, no conversation with others, all alone.
Isolated from spouse, family, friends, now unknown.
Naked, humiliating shame, can't hide.
Vulnerable, stripped of all honor and pride.

Deeper levels of hell, higher degree of wickedness and sin.
The worst depraved souls, more severe punishment herein.
The heartless, immoral, sacrilegious, arrogant, evil doers.
Graduate to eternal damnation in Hades sewers.

Giant creatures, 15 feet tall, stout and strong.
Ugly large teeth, scales, fins and claws so long.
Demon-angels speaking in unknown tongues, blasphemous hatred.
Unmerciful eyes directed at man in God's image, spitting putrid.

Evil monsters, ripping chests, crushing heads, terminating torment.
Enjoy another's miserable suffering for amusement.
Human wounds, no sweat, no pus, no blood.
Real inflicted hurt, no bodily fluids flood.

Cell walls, a thousand crawling slimy reptiles, the living dead.
Huge rats, spiders, maggots and snakes overhead.
Devil-like, decomposing deceivers poised to attack.
Inject penetrating evil and poison in your back.

No hope for mental peace.
Dread and screams shall increase.
Frightful fear of horrors to come.
Crave evil judgment to be done.

Sinful soul on the verge of insanity.
Welcome relief shall not come throughout infinity.
Unsaved sinners thrown into fiery pits of hell.
Like the persecuted Holocaust Jews in burning ovens yell.

Coffin, dirt, as if buried alive.
Pray to finish death and never survive.
Endless desire to rest and die.
A crucifying eternity to terrify.

Pits of fire, burning sinners, clawing to get out.
Shrieking, screaming, crying, a pitiful shout.
A hundred fiery holes, the abyss, hopeless non-believers to blame.
Trapped forever, no escape from the blazing feeding flame.

Suddenly, a pure white sunburst guiding light.
Shines down into the pit of dark night.
A shepherd's voice calling for his lost lamb.
I asked, "Jesus?" He replied, "I am!"

I took His hand and thanked Him!
Praised Him over and over again!
We ascended together to the welcome sky!
Hell was real, but I did not die!

WHAT TO DO IF LEFT BEHIND

You wake up one morning.
Discover your underage children missing.
TV breaking news screaming.
Millions of people worldwide disappearing.

Airplanes with no pilots, crashing.
Cars and trains, no drivers, smashing.
Business offices, few people, no working.
Homes with family members dissolving.

Ministers gone, no preaching.
Doctors and even lawyers, vanishing.
Police and firemen lacking.
Restaurants without cooks, no eating.

Schools vacant, no teaching.
Government offices void, no leading.
Churches empty, no praying.
Athletes absent, no sports playing.

You wake your wife –
"We need now to discuss our afterlife.
Everybody's gone – Is this that rapture thing?
Where Jesus snatches His people everlasting –
Our Christian friends warned us about?
We weren't ready and had some doubt."
Then you call your best friend –
No answer, he's raptured to Heaven you comprehend.

"So, it's true! Jesus was the moral educator,
The Son of God, our creator.
He died on the cross
To save our sins from chaos.

He rose again from the dead,
Like the Bible said.
If we believe in Him,
And repent of all our sin,
We will go to Heaven."

"Do you think it's too late?
Oh! Why did we wait?
Let's drop to our knees.
Pray to accept Christ, if you please.
We were so blind.
We've been left behind.
Praise God a love song.
Admit to Him we were wrong."

Will God hear a last minute call for salvation
To avoid hell and the 7 year tribulation?
Absolutely! God is merciful and forgiving.
He wants all His children in Heaven living.
It's not too late! Pray to Him who forgave.
"Whoever calls on the name of the Lord shall be saved."

BELIEVE!

When you say goodbye and die!
Will your dark soul sigh and testify to terrify
As you disqualify and sink to nullify and mortify?
Or will your loving heart fly to the heavenly sky
To spiritually reunify, purify and glorify?

It's so easy to believe!
Don't leave Earth with grieve and misconceive.
It only takes one second to receive -
Accept Jesus Christ's saving, repenting reprieve,
And God's eternal life award achieve.
It's the right thing to do - BELIEVE!

HOW TO BELIEVE!

Believe and receive Jesus Christ as your Savior Now!
Pray this prayer – I'll show you how!
Seek a sincere attitude in your loving heart,
Speak aloud these exact words – Begin and start:

"Lord Jesus, thank you for loving me!
Open my humble heart so I can truly receive!
I need you today,
Wash all my sins away!"

"Thank you Lord, for dying on the cross,
Paying for all my sins to toss!
Thank you Lord, for rising from the dead,
Only thru you can I enter God's homestead!"

"I open the door of my heart and life right now,
Accept you as my Savior, Lord, and bow!
Thank you for my eternal existence and forgiving all my sin,
Change my life, fill me with your Holy Spirit, Amen!"

"Please take control of my life, teach me,
Make me the kind of person you want me to be!
I love you and want to follow you wherever,
So I can please and serve you forever!"

If you prayed with sincere faith and inspiration –
In Christ's death and resurrection, congratulations!
Into God's family you are forever adopted!
Be happy and joyfully contented!

You are now a new spiritual creature,
By believing in Jesus Christ, the Holy teacher!
In Christ "the old things passed away,"
". . . New things have come" to stay!

You are now a child of God thru faith in Jesus Christ,
Your destiny after death is eternal paradise!
All the resurrected souls and angels in Heaven
Are rejoicing for a repenting sinner forgiven!

Leave your earthly worries and misery behind,
You now have a supernatural peace of mind!
God's Holy Spirit lives within you!
By believing – your salvation is sealed, the message is true!

All followers of Jesus Christ have everlasting hope,
A steady anchor of courage, strength and wisdom to cope!
You are now a Christ Believer, shout it to all others,
Your believing and non-believing sisters and brothers!

Wasn't that so simple?
Live forever in the Holy Temple!
Welcome to the club as a Christ Believer!
Enjoy perfect eternity as a God Receiver!
. . . Amen and Amen!

                                    In Christ,
                                    J. Robert Stump ✝

www.ingramcontent.com/pod-product-compliance
Lightning Source LLC
LaVergne TN
LVHW051842080426
835512LV00018B/3023